# Midnight memories in twilight hours
# And slumbering thoughts

**David Christopher Bussell Lawrence**

Published by New Generation Publishing in 2021



First Edition



ISBN 978-1-80031-250-0

**www.newgeneration-publishing.com**

# These proses

## Midnight memories in the twilight hours
## And slumbering thoughts

These prose or verses are written as a form of release, an opening of my heart as well as my mind, a kind of relief of the inner thoughts within me.

To attempt to explain each and every one of them would be extremely difficult, almost impossible, yet for me they are something of the late at night, early morning feelings that I am sure are felt by many more people, than just myself.

Read them, please enjoy them, make of them what you will.

Thank you to my wonderful Carole, for your help and understanding during all the years, my best friend.

Other books by this author David Lawrence
A Chance Meeting
The Dawn of Togetherness
The Reward of Time
A Second Chance

# Contents

# A night to forget

Sometimes, this sanctuary doesn't even give me that. It reveals my own weaknesses, not strong enough to answer to my eldest son,

"What do you want?"
when I feel as if everything, I do is wrong.

Sunday 05.01.2014.
Yes you come to mind!

I want someone's shoulder to cry on, someone detached from the situation, not my wonderful understanding wife, my Mum.

Did I ever make you feel this way? Our strengths were the same, as much as our weaknesses, did we ever go home leaving you wanting?

I guess the answer must be yes!

This place will be standing long after I have gone, will either of the boys or girls have the same feelings as I have had for this place of safety?

That is a question that will be a long time in answering!

# A shoulder to cry on

A shoulder to cry on

There are times in ones life
When some tasks become too much
The strain too much
Too bare alone

But that shoulder is so far away
No touch will bring it near
Yet still you long for that time
Time when life was rosy

When that shoulder
Was always close

# A voice of comfort

Alone in the night I hear you call
You call to me as you did when you were here
Your voice rings in that familiar manner
It gives me comfort

Are you still there?
When I'm alone and need your guidance
Will you be long?
I hear you ask

Dinner is ready
You call once more
Our names are on your tongue
But you are not here

The past remains
We move on
But to what end
It will come around

If places could speak
I could have endless conversations
Ron, David!
Will you be long?

# Am I to spend my time?

Am I to spend my time?
Asking questions of myself
The answers I can no longer give

I relive the past
The details graphic and real
Time does not ease the pain
Nor should it

My foolish mistakes give way to anger
For not believing what my head does tell

# Another day

Another day
Another fight
With an unwilling participant
Too take part
In one of life's
Daily rituals

# Answers

If
I knew the answers to all the questions
I would never have written many of the questions

Then sometimes the answers
Are far more painful than the questions

But if you don't ask the question
You may never get to the truth

As painful as it can be to accept the truth
It may be better to be hurt now
Rather than elude oneself for a lifetime

# Conversations

Conversations from the past come to mind
Disfigured as well as unkind
Struggle to interpret what was implied

Yet all the time knowing the truth
The pictures in the mind differ
So much from what went on

And still I struggle to recall
So many
Conversations

# Different

We are as individual
As each day that changes
As it unfolds
Never the same day
Twice

# Dreams

My dreams are of the past
The distant rosy past

But not all of the past is rosy
Not by any standard

I have at times behaved badly
Towards many

Younger days provided
Incorrect opportunities

Now the hand in a wrong place
The broken promise

These events don't appear in my dreams
Maybe nightmares for others

At times the past comes back to haunt
Guilty feelings replace the rosy glow

The not so distant past
That is how it feels at times
Not so rosy for others

# Early morning mental ramblings

Confused by excessive drinking
Lost chances linger in the mind
Regrets?
Only for the doings of the night before

I search for past reasons
Why I behave so badly towards myself
I have so much
Yet want even more
More of what I'm not entitled to

I lay wondering what I said
Worse
What I didn't say
My actions are hard to recall
All for the enjoyment of drink

The hours pass with broken sleep
I must give it a rest
I mentally tell myself
Why do I fool myself?

It has to be all
Or nothing
No halfway measures
Stop or it will stop me

# Elements of the past

If we could break down the past
Into sections
Would it help?
Help to understand the things we've done

The past has many tentacles
Like the layers of an onion
As we peel one away
Another is reveiled

So our time may be short
But our past can be deep
Rewarding?
Maybe

But to whom
The tentacles have ways of reminding us
The tap on the shoulder
The flash of memory

All there to make us recall
The things we've said and done
Somewhere in the
Distant past

# Freedom

This freedom comes at a price
Count ourselves lucky we can complain

We have the option to change our paths
Others are not so fortunate

Outspoken views
Sometimes lead to the ultimate sacrifice

Others have paid the cost for us to grumble
Some hide behind this hard-fought freedom

# Guilty

Guilty of being the person that I am not
That's how they find me
Do this
Go there

You don't want to do that
Go there why?
Keep up
Never too old

Never asking what I want
It doesn't matter
When you are guilty of being the person
That you are not

# I guess

I guess I will never see you again
Only in my dreams

If we were to meet
What would I say?

I dream of you
Would seem most inappropriate

Do I miss you?
Well as I never really knew you

The answer must be...
Unknown

# I met a man in the city

At a time
When I was younger
I met a man in the city
He became my friend

I met his wife
And two small children
Our friendship grew
As I too grew

My life changed
As did his advice
He was the best man
The best a couple could ask for

Always wise and strong
Yet at the same time reserved
Watching from the side lines
His wisdom with him

Now time brings challenges
But the love I have is strong
No debts to pay
Actions of love to show

To bring rewards of their-own
Kindness to repay
The years passed by
I like to think
That I too am wiser

## Inside tears

The times we see no one
Are they the times we shed inside tears?
Mine alone no one to comfort me
Thoughts from long ago
The child's smile in return for a gift

Soothing words from mother
Drunken rage from father
What do I miss the most?

Everyday a wish to have my mother
The happy times
Not the bad

Mine are often
Only they are deep inside of me
Alone it is hard to forget
The pain that cause these tears

I miss the feel
I miss the touch
Comfort from a caring hand
One day!
We'll be together
Again

# Is it the fear?

The fear of loosing the one you love, or
The fear of loosing the one that does so much for you.

Can you comprehend the future without that person?
Or is that what fuels the fear?

When I was alone, it was the love I missed
The lonely nights
Empty spaces
The soul mate
My lack of completeness

So used to being a part of something
I couldn't place in my mind
But you had been with me for so long
Our dreams

The plans we'd made together seemed to slip away into
the darkness of the night.
To wake and I was alone
You so far away
Beyond reach

Yet still here
In my mind

# Love

Unseen
Unable to touch
Unable to hear
Yet it is all around

At times all consuming
Overpowering
Unstoppable
It drives us on

Yet it is unseen
A commodity with no shape or size
It has no colour
No smell

It is a feeling
Between a man and a woman
Or a man and a man
Between a human and an animal
An untouchable feeling

Is it only a word?
A word that will make you cry
Sometimes unrequited
And that brings pain

But love cannot be measured
It has no depth
No length
No height

Perhaps used to often
Is it that cheap a word?

# Mother

I miss you for my friend
The only one that knew my ways
You made me
Gave birth to me
And more

Sometimes I ask if you are still there
Of course you are
To me and many more
The hurt is no more

But the missing goes on
You understood my every move
You may not have approved
But to understand
Is above this man's own challenge

And at your end
I too was there
Part
Rather a lot of me also ended
The remainder carries on
Without you

# My confessional place

This my confessional place

Is one of the places that are at times very private to me
Together with my own personal diary

They are open to know one
These details are for the relief of my inner being

When examined by others
They will reveal the weakness that is every part of me

And possibly many others
All be it unknown to themselves
At the time

# My Mind

My mind is like a cluttered box
Full of life's jagged emotions
Love
Life
Fear

Like a jigsaw waiting to be assembled
But
The corners do not fit together
A scrabble in the night trying to mould them into place
The result
Fragmented sleep

Clutching at past dreams
Would-be thoughts and expired wishes
Shake the un-waking hours
Alone in the night a voice inside your head calls

It comes from that lonely space inside your head
That you occupy
Sweet dreams seem so far away

A look at the dark ceiling
Brings more empty thoughts
This torment lingers into the lighting hours

Daylight and the morning brings partial relief
But
These anguished thoughts linger on
Until the soberness returns

# Not far away

Not far away I stand and remember
Remember you
And all your kindness
You took with you when you left

Left alone
With only memories
Memories of love
Love and kindness

Only to remember
At times I need you so much
To get me through
These difficult times

Times when I feel so alone
My past comes to get me
Get me from behind
Only you would understand

That is when I need you most
To reassure
Give confidence
Ease my insecurities

# Of the Place

Of the place
(After Billy)

Nothing is the same
But it is
It is us that change, hang on to the past
Reasons seem unclear
It is in our minds

A reluctance to let go
We hold on to a comfortable dream
The way it has always been, we tell ourselves
Why let go

For we can dream

Dreaming is comforting
Soothing to the inner soul
Memories of the past seem complete
At times they block out any pain

I miss you Billy as I knew I would
You're late night call
You're presence in the room
The playful morning role on the carpet

I guess it comes down once again
To inside tears

# Paths of history

We tread the paths of history
Sometime unknown to ourselves
Those before have placed their feet
Some belonging to us
Many unknown

When enlightened
We stand mesmerised
My father before me
Grandfather too

Not the same for us!
Just a different placing
Of our feet

These paths continue
For all of history
Just different feet
As well as different times

That is the paths of history

# Remember

Well

That old thorn in my side
Every time I say forget
I find a reason to remember

So it is well
To remember that old thorn
Or is it?

## The distant past

The distant past
It conjures mixed feelings
Pleasant at first
Then sad beyond

Carefree abandon
No shackles to tie
Life's easy path

But hidden beneath stones unturned
Secrets we would rather forget
The pain of disappointment
Broken promises

Happiness
Is only what you want to remember?
Within the confine of our minds
We carry turmoil
And hurt

And hide them
Under the mental stones

# The dreams

The dreams are vivid and real
With actions alive with desire and wishes
Beyond my waking thoughts
You are not away
It is almost the here and now

Awaking brings the past back
Reliving the nights recollections
Thoughts of never was
Wishes of it could have been

Never confined to the refuse side of my mind
A warm feeling once again engulfs my being
As a person you were real
But my dreams are not so

## The measures we go too

Beside ourselves with deceit
We try any move to get away with our unhealthy desire
Blind to the pain and anguish we will inflict

Yet still something drives us on
The unknowing
Some hidden desire
Deep in the mind

It blinds out thoughts
Taking reality away
False hopes
Conceived in the mind
Are never given up

# The quietness

The quietness of a Christmas morning
Early
When nothing stirs

Now alone with just a Robin's song for company
This Christmas will be like no other
As all the previous have been

Never two the same
One after the other they speed by

By the time the next is here
The last is barely forgotten
Grumbles of it used to be better

Mean nothing to the future
The past is a long way behind us
Is it progress?

# The secrets we carry

The secrets we carry
That late night call
No message to leave
No one
But all!

Maybe each one of us has been there
In reality
In dreams

The fear of being found out
The what if
Brings doubt

I'm like many
But also the few

# The valley of life

Looking down the past
It's reminiscent of the by-gone past

Life
It comes to haunt
Tugs at thoughts
Makes reflection rosey

The past glowing red
No fear of what is to come
But the now becomes the past

And the future the now
It's not always easy to forget
But do we learn from what went on

The answer is hard to find
Hidden beneath a long time ago
Blankets of dreams and wishes fall away

The same as night becomes day
Leaving an uncovered innocence

Reality kicks in
Life moves on

The valleys are a thing of the past

Only visited on silent days
Or dark slumbering nights

## The weakness

The weakness that takes on strength of its own
Knows no difference between right and wrong
My anger
My rage
Jealousy

Replaced by foolish actions
Trying to impress
Clouded judgement
A collapse of rightfulness

Never to say ones true
Feelings

The recovering addict
That is one fix, drink or bet away from complete ruination
If they give in

The weakness will then take on its own complete
overpowering strength
In the end this strength will overcome

Destroy the very being
Bring complete confusion
A mind and life shot away

# The wind that blows

On the wind I felt my fate
Cold on my back
And a chill to the core

Worse than threats
It brings bad news
Like daggers that pierce
Deeper than the surface

Frozen with fear
I turn to look
But no one there
It blows again

Just to remind
It's always there
Behind you
That tap on the back

# These artefacts

The cups from a faraway place
Bring thoughts from the past
But only happy for the owners
To others they are tat

The memories are not written down with the article
They are stored in the mind of the original owner

# This Past

This past that places its hand on your shoulder
You turn to look
Sure you're in the right place
But the time is now

The years have changed the surroundings
But your mind only recalls your past
Happy or sad you long for it back

The way it was
Or you thought it was

You shake hands with a distant memory
Farewell

Until the next time
Then other thoughts will come to trace a path

To the distant beginnings
Of your past
Farewell

And the future will become the past in time
Then often we will recall
Those last farewells

# This wounded heart!

This wounded heart
The scar that runs so deep
Its healing path that never completes
Opened again by time
Somewhat self-inflicted
This wounded heart

The scar that runs so deep
Below the surface and beyond
It opens with ease at the thought of you
Bleeding feelings and distress to the open world
The scar that runs so deep

Its healing path that never completes
Pain brought about by contemplation
Actions beyond understanding of the level mind
Looking for a reason to repair the hurt
Its healing path that never completes

Opened again by time
The sound of the voice
The soothing presence of those tones
But not for the one that wishes an understanding
Opened again by time

Somewhat self-inflicted
The lure of a telephone on a cold dark night
In the hand the buttons are pressed
The voice that can do no wrong
Again, a question asked
With no response
Somewhat self-inflicted

This wounded heart
The scar that runs so deep
Its healing path that never completes
Opened again by time
Somewhat self-inflicted

# Unable to sleep

Unable to sleep you lie awake
The sound of the night strong
The slightest of movements stir
The pipes that click

You wait for the unexpected
But it doesn't come
The mind wonders
The ifs
Become maybe's

The haves
A lost memory

The clock ticks
The darkness draws on and on
You long for the daylight
The dawn!

Come morning
The night has gone
But not the lost sleep that you yearn

Come tonight
The same returns

# What would I give?

What would I give?
For one more conversation
On the phone
Or in person

Just to hear your voice
Words of comfort
Reassurance on a cold wet night
When thoughts are low
In need of alleviation

At times I feel so alone
When all around me are happy
I find no solace in others joy
What would I give?
Just one more time

www.ingramcontent.com/pod-product-compliance
Ingram Content Group UK Ltd.
Pitfield, Milton Keynes, MK11 3LW, UK
UKHW042001190726
13854UKWH00005B/2103

9 781800 312500